Easy Pass

Site	Username	Password

Easy Password Tracker

Site	Username	Password

Easy Password Tracker

Site	Username	Password

Easy Password Tracker

Site	Username	Password

Easy Password Tracker

Site	Username	Password

Easy Password Tracker

Site	Username	Password

Easy Password Tracker

Site	Username	Password

Easy Password Tracker

Site	Username	Password

Easy Password Tracker

Site	Username	Password

Easy Password Tracker

Site	Username	Password

Easy Password Tracker

Site	Username	Password

Easy Password Tracker

Site	Username	Password

Easy Password Tracker

Site	Username	Password

Easy Password Tracker

Site	Username	Password

Easy Password Tracker

Site	Username	Password

Easy Password Tracker

Site	Username	Password

Easy Password Tracker

Site	Username	Password

Easy Password Tracker

Site	Username	Password

Easy Password Tracker

Site	Username	Password

Easy Password Tracker

Site	Username	Password

Easy Password Tracker

Site	Username	Password

Easy Password Tracker

Site	Username	Password

Easy Password Tracker

Site	Username	Password

Easy Password Tracker

Site	Username	Password

Easy Password Tracker

Site	Username	Password

Easy Password Tracker

Site	Username	Password

Easy Password Tracker

Site	Username	Password

Easy Password Tracker

Site	Username	Password

Easy Password Tracker

Site	Username	Password

Easy Password Tracker

Site	Username	Password

Easy Password Tracker

Site	Username	Password

Easy Password Tracker

Site	Username	Password

Easy Password Tracker

Site	Username	Password

Easy Password Tracker

Site	Username	Password

Easy Password Tracker

Site	Username	Password

Easy Password Tracker

Site	Username	Password

Easy Password Tracker

Site	Username	Password

Easy Password Tracker

Site	Username	Password

Easy Password Tracker

Site	Username	Password

Easy Password Tracker

Site	Username	Password

Easy Password Tracker

Site	Username	Password

Easy Password Tracker

Site	Username	Password

Easy Password Tracker

Site	Username	Password

Easy Password Tracker

Site	Username	Password

Easy Password Tracker

Site	Username	Password

Easy Password Tracker

Site	Username	Password

Easy Password Tracker

Site	Username	Password

Easy Password Tracker

Site	Username	Password

Easy Password Tracker

Site	Username	Password

Easy Password Tracker

Site	Username	Password

Easy Password Tracker

Site	Username	Password

Easy Password Tracker

Site	Username	Password

Easy Password Tracker

Site	Username	Password

Easy Password Tracker

Site	Username	Password

Easy Password Tracker

Site	Username	Password

Easy Password Tracker

Site	Username	Password

Easy Password Tracker

Site	Username	Password

Easy Password Tracker

Site	Username	Password

Easy Password Tracker

Site	Username	Password

Easy Password Tracker

Site	Username	Password

Easy Password Tracker

Site	Username	Password

Easy Password Tracker

Site	Username	Password

Easy Password Tracker

Site	Username	Password

Easy Password Tracker

Site	Username	Password

Easy Password Tracker

Site	Username	Password

Easy Password Tracker

Site	Username	Password

Easy Password Tracker

Site	Username	Password

Easy Password Tracker

Site	Username	Password

Easy Password Tracker

Site	Username	Password

Easy Password Tracker

Site	Username	Password

Easy Password Tracker

Site	Username	Password

Easy Password Tracker

Site	Username	Password

Easy Password Tracker

Site	Username	Password

Easy Password Tracker

Site	Username	Password

Easy Password Tracker

Site	Username	Password

Easy Password Tracker

Site	Username	Password

Easy Password Tracker

Site	Username	Password

Easy Password Tracker

Site	Username	Password

Easy Password Tracker

Site	Username	Password

Easy Password Tracker

Site	Username	Password

Easy Password Tracker

Site	Username	Password

Easy Password Tracker

Site	Username	Password

Easy Password Tracker

Site	Username	Password

Easy Password Tracker

Site	Username	Password

Easy Password Tracker

Site	Username	Password

Easy Password Tracker

Site	Username	Password

Easy Password Tracker

Site	Username	Password

Easy Password Tracker

Site	Username	Password

Easy Password Tracker

Site	Username	Password

Easy Password Tracker

Site	Username	Password

Easy Password Tracker

Site	Username	Password

Easy Password Tracker

Site	Username	Password

Easy Password Tracker

Site	Username	Password

Easy Password Tracker

Site	Username	Password

Easy Password Tracker

Site	Username	Password

Easy Password Tracker

Site	Username	Password

Easy Password Tracker

Site	Username	Password

Easy Password Tracker

Site	Username	Password

Easy Password Tracker

Site	Username	Password

Easy Password Tracker

Site	Username	Password

Easy Password Tracker

Site	Username	Password

Easy Password Tracker

Site	Username	Password

Easy Password Tracker

Site	Username	Password

Easy Password Tracker

Site	Username	Password

Easy Password Tracker

Site	Username	Password

Easy Password Tracker

Site	Username	Password

Easy Password Tracker

Site	Username	Password

Easy Password Tracker

Site	Username	Password

Easy Password Tracker

Site	Username	Password

Easy Password Tracker

Site	Username	Password

Easy Password Tracker

Site	Username	Password

Easy Password Tracker

Site	Username	Password

Easy Password Tracker

Site	Username	Password

Easy Password Tracker

Site	Username	Password

Easy Password Tracker

Site	Username	Password

Easy Password Tracker

Site	Username	Password

Easy Password Tracker

Site	Username	Password

Easy Password Tracker

Site	Username	Password

Easy Password Tracker

Site	Username	Password

Easy Password Tracker

Site	Username	Password

Printed in Great Britain
by Amazon

43103646R00069